STARTUP STRATEGIES

I0427285

Navigating Success in the New Business Landscape

NANCY BARLOW

TABLE OF CONTENT

INTRODUCTION

In the ever-evolving world of entrepreneurship, navigating the landscape of startups has become increasingly complex and challenging. As the global economy continues to shift, driven by technological advancements, changing consumer behaviors, and unprecedented market dynamics, the traditional playbook for launching and scaling a startup no longer guarantees success. Instead, entrepreneurs must adapt to a new reality—one defined by uncertainty, disruption, and fierce competition.

Welcome to "Startup Strategies: Navigating Success in the New Business Landscape." In this book, we embark on a journey through the intricacies of modern entrepreneurship, offering a comprehensive guide for aspiring and seasoned entrepreneurs alike. Drawing on years of experience, extensive research, and insights from industry experts, this book serves as a roadmap for startups aiming not just to survive but to thrive in today's dynamic environment.

The traditional barriers to entry have crumbled, allowing startups to emerge from anywhere in the world and disrupt established industries seemingly overnight. However, with this unprecedented opportunity comes unprecedented challenges. Startups must navigate a myriad of obstacles, from securing funding in a competitive investment landscape to building a resilient team capable of adapting to rapid change.

Moreover, the COVID-19 pandemic has reshaped the business landscape in ways previously unimaginable, accelerating digital transformation and altering consumer preferences indefinitely. As such, startups must embrace agility and innovation to remain relevant and competitive in this new era.

Throughout this book, we delve into essential topics such as identifying market opportunities, crafting a compelling value proposition, building a robust business model, and executing effective go-to-market strategies. We also explore the importance of fostering a strong company culture, nurturing talent, and leveraging technology to drive sustainable growth.

Whether you're a first-time entrepreneur brimming with ideas or a seasoned startup founder looking to recalibrate your approach, "Startup Strategies" equips you with the knowledge, tools, and strategies needed to thrive in today's rapidly evolving business landscape. Join us as we embark on this transformative journey together, where innovation meets execution, and success knows no bounds.

CHAPTER 1:
UNDERSTANDING THE
NEW BUSINESS
LANDSCAPE

In the fast-paced world of entrepreneurship, success hinges not only on the brilliance of your idea or the strength of your execution but also on your ability to navigate the ever-changing terrain of the business landscape. Chapter 1 of "Startup Strategies: Navigating Success in the New Business Landscape" lays the groundwork by providing a comprehensive overview of the forces shaping today's business environment.

The modern business landscape is a dynamic ecosystem shaped by a myriad of factors, including technological advancements, shifting market trends, and evolving consumer behaviors. In this chapter, we embark on a journey to dissect these key elements, offering insights and analysis to help entrepreneurs understand the intricacies of the new business terrain.

We start by examining the profound impact of technology on the way businesses operate and compete. From the rise of artificial intelligence and automation to the growing influence of big data analytics and blockchain technology, we explore how these innovations are reshaping industries and disrupting traditional business models.

Furthermore, we delve into the shifting dynamics of market trends and consumer behavior, emphasizing the importance of staying attuned to emerging trends and anticipating changing customer needs. In today's hyper-connected world, where consumer preferences can shift overnight and viral trends can catapult unknown startups to fame, understanding the pulse of the market is more critical than ever.

Finally, we address the challenges and opportunities facing startups in this new landscape, from fierce competition and regulatory hurdles to the democratization of entrepreneurship and the rise of global markets. By gaining a deeper understanding of the forces at play, entrepreneurs can better position themselves to seize opportunities, mitigate risks, and chart a course toward sustainable success.

As we embark on this exploration of the new business landscape, I invite you to open your mind to the possibilities and challenges that lie ahead. By equipping yourself with the knowledge and insights offered in this chapter, you'll be better prepared to navigate the complexities of modern entrepreneurship and steer your startup toward a prosperous future.

- The forces shaping the modern business environment

The modern business environment is shaped by a multitude of forces, both internal and external, that influence how companies operate, compete, and innovate. Understanding these forces is essential for businesses to adapt, thrive, and maintain a competitive edge. Here's a comprehensive discussion of the key forces shaping the modern business environment:

1. **Technological Advancements**:

   - Rapid advancements in technology, such as artificial intelligence (AI), machine learning, automation, and the Internet of Things (IoT), are revolutionizing industries and business processes.

   - Technology enables companies to streamline operations, enhance productivity, and create innovative products and services.

   - Digital transformation has become imperative, with businesses leveraging technology to optimize customer experiences, personalize marketing efforts, and gain actionable insights from data analytic

2. Globalization:

- The interconnectedness of economies worldwide has led to increased competition, expanded markets, and the emergence of multinational corporations.

- Globalization offers opportunities for businesses to access new markets, tap into diverse talent pools, and leverage economies of scale.

- However, globalization also presents challenges, such as navigating complex international regulations, managing cultural differences, and mitigating geopolitical risks.

3. Changing Consumer Behavior:

- Consumer preferences and behaviors are constantly evolving, driven by factors such as demographic shifts, socio-cultural trends, and technological advancements.

- Consumers increasingly demand personalized experiences, seamless Omni channel interactions, and socially responsible products and brands.

- Businesses must stay agile and responsive to changing consumer expectations, leveraging data analytics and market research to anticipate and meet consumer needs effectively.

4. Regulatory and Legal Environment:

- Businesses operate within a framework of laws, regulations, and government policies that shape industry standards, competition, and market dynamics.

- Regulatory compliance is essential for businesses to mitigate legal risks, ensure ethical conduct, and maintain public trust.

- The regulatory landscape is constantly evolving, with new laws and regulations emerging in response to societal concerns, technological advancements, and economic developments.

5. Socio-Economic Trends:

- Socio-economic trends, such as demographic shifts, urbanization, income inequality, and environmental sustainability, profoundly impact businesses and industries.

- Businesses must address societal challenges, such as climate change and social justice, by adopting sustainable practices, corporate social responsibility (CSR) initiatives, and ethical business practices.

- Consumer preferences are increasingly influenced by ethical considerations, driving demand for environmentally friendly products, fair labor practices, and transparent supply chains.

6. **Competitive Dynamics:**

- Intense competition prevails across industries, fueled by globalization, technological innovation, and disruptive startups.

- Businesses must continuously innovate, differentiate their offerings, and enhance operational efficiency to gain a competitive advantage.

- Collaboration and strategic partnerships can also be effective strategies for businesses to strengthen their market position and expand their reach.

In conclusion, the modern business environment is characterized by dynamic and interconnected forces that shape industry landscapes, market dynamics, and business strategies. To thrive in this environment, businesses must embrace innovation, agility, and strategic foresight to adapt to changing trends, anticipate future challenges, and seize emerging opportunities.

- Analyzing the impact of technological advancements, market trends, and consumer behavior shifts

Analyzing the impact of technological advancements, market trends, and consumer behavior shifts is a crucial process for businesses to understand the evolving landscape in which they operate. This analysis provides insights that enable companies to make informed decisions, identify opportunities for innovation, and stay ahead of the competition. Here's a comprehensive discussion of the process:

1. **Identifying Key Technological Advancements:**

   - Begin by identifying the latest technological advancements relevant to your industry. This could include breakthroughs in AI, machine learning, blockchain, IoT, or robotics.

- Evaluate how these technologies are being adopted and integrated into various business processes, products, and services.

- Assess the potential impact of these advancements on your industry, such as increased automation, improved efficiency, or disruption of traditional business models.

2. **Assessing Market Trends**:

- Conduct market research to identify current trends shaping your industry. This may involve analyzing industry reports, competitor strategies, and consumer surveys.

- Look for emerging trends in consumer preferences, purchasing behavior, and market demand. Pay attention to shifts in demographics, socio-cultural norms, and economic factors.

- Evaluate how these trends are influencing market dynamics, competitive landscape, and business opportunities. Determine whether they present threats or opportunities for your organization.

3. **Monitoring Consumer Behavior Shifts**:

  - Utilize data analytics tools to track and analyze consumer behavior across various channels, including online platforms, social media, and retail stores.

  - Segment your target audience based on demographic, psychographic, and behavioral factors to gain a deeper understanding of their preferences, needs, and pain points.

  - Identify patterns, trends, and anomalies in consumer behavior, such as changing purchase patterns, product preferences, or brand loyalty.

  - Explore the underlying drivers behind these shifts, such as changes in lifestyle, technological adoption, or cultural influences.

4. **Quantifying Impact and Implications**:

- Quantify the potential impact of technological advancements, market trends, and consumer behavior shifts on your business operations, revenue streams, and competitive position.

- Assess the implications for various aspects of your business, including product development, marketing strategies, supply chain management, and customer engagement.

- Consider both short-term and long-term effects, as well as potential risks and opportunities associated with each trend or shift.

5. **Adapting Strategies and Initiatives**:

- Based on your analysis, develop strategies and initiatives to capitalize on opportunities and mitigate risks arising from technological advancements, market trends, and consumer behavior shifts.

- Prioritize investments in areas that align with emerging trends and consumer preferences, such as innovation, digital transformation, and customer experience enhancements.

- Continuously monitor and reassess your analysis to stay agile and responsive to evolving market dynamics and consumer needs.

6. **Iterative Process of Analysis and Action:**

- Recognize that analyzing the impact of technological advancements, market trends, and consumer behavior shifts is an iterative process that requires ongoing monitoring, analysis, and adaptation.

- Stay vigilant for new developments and changes in the business environment, and be prepared to adjust your strategies and initiatives accordingly.

- Foster a culture of innovation and learning within your organization to effectively navigate and capitalize on the opportunities presented by the evolving landscape.

In conclusion, analyzing the impact of technological advancements, market trends, and consumer behavior shifts is a multifaceted process that requires a combination of data-driven analysis, strategic foresight, and agility. By understanding how these factors influence your business, you can make informed decisions, drive innovation, and maintain a competitive edge in an ever-changing marketplace.

- Identifying opportunities and challenges for startups in the current landscape

Identifying opportunities and challenges for startups in the current landscape is a critical process that involves thorough analysis, strategic thinking, and a deep understanding of market dynamics. Here's a comprehensive discussion of the process:

1. Market Research and Analysis:

- Start by conducting comprehensive market research to identify industry trends, customer needs, and competitive dynamics.

- Analyze market size, growth potential, and key players to assess the viability of entering the market.

- Identify niche markets or underserved segments where your startup can differentiate itself and create value.

2. SWOT Analysis:

- Conduct a SWOT (Strengths, Weaknesses, Opportunities, Threats) analysis to assess your startup's internal capabilities and external factors.

- Identify your startup's strengths and unique selling points that can be leveraged to seize opportunities.

- Recognize potential weaknesses and threats that could hinder your startup's growth or pose challenges in the market.

3. Emerging Trends and Technologies:

- Stay informed about emerging trends, technological advancements, and industry disruptors that could create new opportunities for startups.

- Evaluate how these trends may impact consumer behavior, market demand, and business models.

- Determine how your startup can capitalize on these trends by offering innovative solutions or leveraging new technologies.

4. Customer Validation:

- Engage with potential customers to validate your startup idea and gather feedback on their pain points, preferences, and willingness to pay.

- Conduct surveys, interviews, or focus groups to gain insights into customer needs and validate market demand for your product or service.

- Use customer feedback to refine your value proposition, product features, and go-to-market strategy.

5. Competitive Analysis:

- Analyze the competitive landscape to understand the strengths, weaknesses, and strategies of existing players in the market.

- Identify gaps or inefficiencies in competitors' offerings that your startup can address or improve upon.

- Assess potential barriers to entry, such as high competition, regulatory hurdles, or established incumbents, and develop strategies to overcome them.

6. Financial Viability and Funding Options:

- Evaluate the financial viability of your startup by estimating costs, revenue projections, and potential profitability.

- Determine the funding requirements needed to launch and scale your startup, considering factors such as product development, marketing, and operational expenses.

- Explore funding options such as bootstrapping, angel investors, venture capital, or crowdfunding, based on your startup's stage of development and growth trajectory.

7. Regulatory and Legal Considerations:

- Identify regulatory requirements and legal considerations that may impact your startup, such as industry regulations, intellectual property rights, and data privacy laws.

- Ensure compliance with relevant regulations and obtain necessary licenses or permits to operate legally.

- Anticipate potential legal challenges or risks that could arise and develop strategies to mitigate them proactively.

8. Talent Acquisition and Team Building:

- Assess the talent and skills needed to drive your startup's success and build a diverse team with complementary expertise.

- Identify key hires, such as technical specialists, marketing professionals, or business development experts, to strengthen your startup's capabilities.

- Develop a culture of collaboration, innovation, and continuous learning to attract and retain top talent.

9. **Scalability and Growth Strategy**:

- Consider the scalability of your business model and how it can adapt to accommodate growth and expansion.

- Develop a growth strategy that outlines how your startup will acquire customers, enter new markets, and scale operations.

- Identify potential challenges or bottlenecks that may arise during the scaling process and develop strategies to overcome them effectively.

In conclusion, identifying opportunities and challenges for startups in the current landscape is a multifaceted process that requires a combination of market research, strategic analysis, customer validation, and careful planning. By thoroughly assessing market dynamics, competitive factors, and internal capabilities, startups can position themselves for success and navigate the challenges of entrepreneurship more effectively.

CHAPTER 2:
CRAFTING A COMPELLING VALUE PROPOSITION

In the crowded marketplace of today's business landscape, the ability to effectively communicate the unique value your product or service offers is paramount to success. Chapter: Crafting a Compelling Value Proposition delves into the fundamental process of distilling your startup's essence into a clear and compelling message that resonates with your target audience.

A value proposition serves as the cornerstone of your business strategy, defining the promise you make to your customers and articulating why they should choose your offering over alternatives. It encapsulates the benefits, features, and differentiation that set your product or service apart from the competition.

In this chapter, we embark on a journey to explore the art and science of crafting a value proposition that captivates, persuades, and inspires action. We delve into the core principles of value proposition development, providing practical insights and actionable strategies to help startups effectively communicate their unique value proposition to their target market.

Through a combination of theory, case studies, and real-world examples, we uncover the key elements of a compelling value proposition and guide you through the process of creating one for your startup. From understanding customer needs and pain points to articulating your product's benefits and differentiation, we equip you with the tools and frameworks needed to craft a value proposition that resonates with your audience.

Moreover, we explore the importance of iteration, testing, and refinement in the value proposition development process. Recognizing that crafting a compelling value proposition is an iterative journey, we emphasize the value of continuous learning, feedback, and adaptation to ensure that your value proposition remains relevant and compelling in a dynamic market environment.

Whether you're launching a new product, entering a new market, or seeking to differentiate your offering in a crowded industry, mastering the art of value proposition crafting is essential for startup success. Join us as we embark on this exploration of value proposition development, where clarity meets persuasion, and differentiation leads to competitive advantage.

- Defining your unique value proposition in a crowded marketplace

Defining your unique value proposition in a crowded marketplace is essential for capturing the attention of your target audience and differentiating your offering from competitors. It requires a deep understanding of customer needs, market dynamics, and your strengths as a business. Here's a comprehensive discussion of the process:

1. **Understand Your Target Audience**:

- Begin by thoroughly understanding your target audience: their demographics, preferences, pain points, and purchasing behavior.

- Conduct market research, surveys, and interviews to gain insights into what motivates your potential customers and what they value most in a product or service.

- Segment your audience based on common characteristics or needs to tailor your value proposition effectively.

2. **Identify Market Gaps and Opportunities**:

- Analyze the competitive landscape to identify gaps or areas where existing solutions are falling short in meeting customer needs.

- Look for unmet needs, underserved segments, or emerging trends that present opportunities for differentiation and innovation.

- Identify potential niches or segments where your offering can provide unique value and gain a competitive edge.

3. **Articulate Your Unique Selling Points**:

- Determine what sets your product or service apart from competitors and why customers should choose you over alternatives.

- Identify your unique selling points (USPs) – the features, benefits, or qualities that make your offering superior or more desirable.

- Focus on aspects such as quality, performance, affordability, convenience, innovation, or sustainability that resonate with your target audience.

4. Highlight Benefits and Outcomes:

- Emphasize the tangible benefits and outcomes that customers can expect from using your product or service.

- Communicate how your offering solves a problem, fulfills a need, or improves customers' lives in meaningful ways.

- Use language that resonates with your audience and speaks to their aspirations, desires, or pain points.

5. Differentiate From Competitors:

- Identify your competitive advantages and how they distinguish you from competitors.

- Highlight areas where you excel, whether it's product features, service quality, customer experience, pricing, or brand reputation.

- Emphasize what makes you unique and why customers should choose you instead of alternatives.

6. Communicate Clear and Compelling Messaging:

- Craft a concise and compelling value proposition statement that communicates your unique value to customers.

- Keep your messaging simple, easy to understand, and customer-centric, focusing on the benefits and outcomes rather than technical details.

- Test your messaging with target customers to ensure it resonates and effectively captures their attention and interest.

7. Consistently Deliver on Your Promise:

- Ensure that your value proposition aligns with the experience customers have when using your product or service.

- Consistently deliver on your promise by providing high-quality products, excellent customer service, and a seamless user experience.

- Build trust and credibility with your audience by consistently meeting or exceeding their expectations.

In conclusion, defining your unique value proposition in a crowded marketplace requires a strategic approach that combines customer insights, competitive analysis, and clear communication. By identifying what sets you apart, highlighting your strengths, and delivering on your promise, you can effectively differentiate your offering and attract customers in a competitive environment.

- Conducting market research to understand customer needs and preferences

Conducting market research to understand customer needs and preferences is essential for developing products or services that resonate with your target audience and ultimately drive business success. Here's a comprehensive discussion of the process:

1. **Define Research Objectives**:

   - Start by clearly defining the objectives of your market research. What specific questions do you want to answer? What insights are you seeking to gain?

   - Determine the scope of your research, including the target audience, geographic location, and timeframe for data collection.

2. **Identify Target Audience**:

   - Define your target audience based on demographic factors (age, gender, income, education), psychographic traits (lifestyle, values, attitudes), and behavioral characteristics (purchase behavior, usage patterns).

   - Segment your audience into distinct groups based on shared characteristics or needs to tailor your research approach effectively.

3. **Choose Research Methods**:

- Select appropriate research methods based on your objectives, budget, and resources available. Common methods include surveys, interviews, focus groups, observation, and secondary research (using existing data and reports).

- Consider both qualitative and quantitative research approaches to gain a comprehensive understanding of customer needs and preferences.

4. **Develop Research Instruments**:

- Design research instruments such as questionnaires, discussion guides, or observation protocols that align with your research objectives and target audience.

- Ensure that your research instruments are clear, concise, and unbiased to collect accurate and actionable data.

5. **Collect Data:**

- Implement your chosen research methods to collect data from your target audience. This may involve distributing surveys, conducting interviews or focus groups, or observing customer behavior.

- Use multiple data collection points and sources to validate findings and ensure the reliability of your research.

6. Analyze Data:

- Organize and analyze the collected data to identify patterns, trends, and insights related to customer needs and preferences.

- Use statistical analysis tools and techniques to quantify findings from quantitative data and derive actionable insights.

- Interpret qualitative data by identifying themes, sentiments, and underlying motivations expressed by respondents.

7. Extract Key Insights:

- Extract key insights from your data analysis that provide valuable information about customer needs, preferences, pain points, and purchase motivations.

- Identify opportunities for product or service innovation, improvement, or differentiation based on customer feedback and market trends.

- Prioritize insights that have the greatest potential impact on your business objectives and strategic decisions.

8. **Apply Findings to Business Strategy**:

- Translate research findings into actionable strategies and initiatives that align with your business goals and objectives.

- Integrate customer insights into product development, marketing strategies, pricing decisions, and customer experience enhancements.

- Continuously monitor market trends and customer feedback to adapt your strategies and stay responsive to evolving needs and preferences.

9. **Iterate and Improve**:

- Treat market research as an iterative process, continuously gathering feedback and refining your understanding of customer needs and preferences over time.

- Incorporate feedback loops into your business processes to capture ongoing insights and make iterative improvements to your products, services, and customer experiences.

- Stay agile and adaptable in responding to changing market conditions, competitive dynamics, and evolving consumer trends.

In conclusion, conducting market research to understand customer needs and preferences is a foundational step in developing a successful business strategy. By systematically gathering, analyzing, and applying customer insights, businesses can make informed decisions, create products or services that resonate with their target audience, and ultimately drive growth and profitability.

- Developing products or services that solve specific pain points and deliver tangible value

Developing products or services that solve specific pain points and deliver tangible value is crucial for businesses to succeed in today's competitive landscape. By addressing customer needs and offering solutions that genuinely improve their lives, businesses can build loyalty, drive sales, and differentiate themselves from competitors. Here's a comprehensive discussion of the process:

1. **Identify Customer Pain Points**:

   - Start by conducting thorough market research to identify common pain points, challenges, and frustrations experienced by your target audience.

- Utilize a variety of research methods, such as surveys, interviews, and observation, to gather insights into customer needs and pain points.

- Pay attention to both explicit and implicit pain points, including unmet needs, inconveniences, inefficiencies, and frustrations encountered in daily life or specific situations.

2. **Understand Customer Needs and Desires**:

- Gain a deep understanding of customer needs, desires, and aspirations by listening to their feedback, observing their behavior, and empathizing with their experiences.

- Segment your target audience based on shared characteristics, preferences, and behaviors to tailor your product or service offerings effectively.

- Consider the emotional, functional, and social dimensions of customer needs to develop solutions that resonate on multiple levels.

3. **Brainstorm Solutions**:

- Brainstorm potential solutions to address identified pain points and meet customer needs effectively.

- Encourage creativity and innovation within your team by exploring a wide range of ideas and concepts.

- Prioritize solutions that offer unique benefits, are technically feasible, and align with your business objectives and resources.

4. **Prototype and Test:**

- Develop prototypes or minimum viable products (MVPs) to test and validate your proposed solutions with real users.

- Solicit feedback from target customers through user testing, beta testing, or pilot programs to assess usability, functionality, and perceived value.

- Iterate on your prototypes based on user feedback, making refinements and improvements to address identified pain points and enhance user experience.

5. Focus on Value Proposition:

 - Ensure that your products or services deliver tangible value and benefits that address specific customer pain points and fulfill unmet needs.

 - Clearly articulate the value proposition of your offering, emphasizing the unique benefits, features, and outcomes it provides to customers.

 - Communicate the value proposition effectively through marketing messages, product packaging, and user documentation to attract and engage customers.

6. Iterate and Refine:

 - Continuously iterate and refine your products or services based on customer feedback, market insights, and evolving needs.

 - Stay agile and responsive to changing market conditions, technological advancements, and competitive dynamics.

- Foster a culture of continuous improvement and innovation within your organization to drive ongoing product development and enhancement.

7. **Measure Impact and Success**:

- Establish key performance indicators (KPIs) to measure the impact and success of your products or services.

- Track metrics such as customer satisfaction, retention rates, sales growth, and market share to evaluate the effectiveness of your solutions in addressing customer pain points and delivering value.

- Use feedback and data analysis to identify areas for improvement and optimization, ensuring that your products or services continue to meet evolving customer needs and expectations.

In conclusion, developing products or services that solve specific pain points and deliver tangible value requires a customer-centric approach, creativity, and continuous iteration. By understanding customer needs, brainstorming innovative solutions, and iterating based on feedback, businesses can create offerings that resonate with customers and drive sustainable growth and success.

CHAPTER 3: BUILDING A SOLID FOUNDATION: FROM IDEA TO EXECUTION

In the journey of entrepreneurship, the transition from idea to execution is perhaps the most pivotal phase, where dreams meet reality and aspirations transform into tangible outcomes. Chapter: Building a Solid Foundation: From Idea to Execution is dedicated to guiding aspiring entrepreneurs through the critical steps involved in laying the groundwork for a successful startup venture.

Embarking on the path of entrepreneurship requires more than just a great idea; it demands strategic planning, meticulous execution, and unwavering dedication. In this chapter, we delve into the essential elements of building a solid foundation for your startup, from refining your initial concept to laying the groundwork for sustainable growth.

We begin by exploring the genesis of startup ideas and the process of ideation, offering insights into how to generate, evaluate, and validate business concepts effectively. We discuss the importance of identifying market opportunities, understanding customer needs, and assessing the competitive landscape to ensure that your idea has the potential to address real-world problems and create value.

Moving beyond ideation, we delve into the intricacies of crafting a robust business model that aligns with your startup's objectives, revenue streams, and scalability. We explore different business models, from subscription-based models to freemium offerings, and provide guidance on selecting the right model for your venture.

Moreover, we address the critical aspects of executing your startup vision, from assembling a talented team and securing funding to establishing operational processes and building a strong organizational culture. We offer practical tips and strategies for navigating common challenges encountered during the early stages of startup development and laying the groundwork for long-term success.

Throughout this chapter, we emphasize the importance of iteration, resilience, and adaptability in the startup journey. We recognize that building a solid foundation is not a linear process but rather an iterative journey characterized by learning, experimentation, and course correction.

Whether you're a first-time entrepreneur with a bold vision or a seasoned startup founder looking to refine your approach, this chapter serves as a comprehensive guide to building a solid foundation for your startup venture. Join us as we embark on this transformative journey, where ideas take shape, dreams become reality, and success awaits those who dare to pursue it.

- Validating your startup idea through market research and customer feedback

Validating your startup idea through market research and customer feedback is a critical step in the entrepreneurial journey. It involves gathering insights from potential customers to assess the viability, desirability, and market fit of your product or service. Here's a comprehensive discussion of the process:

1. **Define Research Objectives**:

   - Clearly define the objectives of your validation process. What specific questions do you want to answer? What insights are you seeking to gain?

   - Determine the scope of your research, including target audience demographics, geographic location, and timeframe for data collection.

2. Identify Target Audience:

- Define your target audience based on demographic factors (age, gender, income, education), psychographic traits (lifestyle, values, attitudes), and behavioral characteristics (purchasing behavior, usage patterns).

- Segment your audience into distinct groups based on shared characteristics or needs to tailor your research approach effectively.

3. Choose Research Methods:

- Select appropriate research methods based on your objectives, budget, and resources available. Common methods include surveys, interviews, focus groups, and observation.

- Consider both qualitative and quantitative research approaches to gain a comprehensive understanding of customer perceptions and preferences.

4. Develop Research Instruments:

- Design research instruments such as questionnaires, discussion guides, or prototype demos that align with your research objectives and target audience.

- Ensure that your research instruments are clear, concise, and unbiased to collect accurate and actionable data.

5. Conduct Market Research:

- Gather market insights by conducting surveys, interviews, or focus groups with your target audience to assess interest, demand, and willingness to pay for your product or service.

- Explore competitors and alternatives in the market to understand existing solutions, pricing strategies, and customer perceptions.

- Leverage secondary research sources such as industry reports, market trends, and customer reviews to supplement primary research findings.

6. Prototype and Test:

- Develop prototypes or minimum viable products (MVPs) to demonstrate your startup idea and gather feedback from potential customers.

- Conduct user testing, beta testing, or pilot programs to assess usability, functionality, and overall satisfaction with your prototype.

- Iterate on your prototype based on user feedback, making refinements and improvements to address identified pain points and enhance user experience.

7. Analyze Feedback and Data:

- Organize and analyze the collected feedback and data to identify patterns, trends, and insights related to customer perceptions and preferences.

- Use statistical analysis tools and techniques to quantify findings from quantitative data and derive actionable insights.

- Interpret qualitative data by identifying themes, sentiments, and underlying motivations expressed by respondents.

8. **Iterate and Refine**:

- Incorporate feedback and insights from market research and customer feedback into the development and refinement of your startup idea.

- Continuously iterate on your product or service based on user feedback, making adjustments and improvements to better meet customer needs and expectations.

- Stay agile and adaptable in responding to changing market conditions, technological advancements, and competitive dynamics.

9. **Make Informed Decisions**:

- Use validated insights and data to make informed decisions about the direction, positioning, and feasibility of your startup idea.

- Determine whether there is sufficient market demand and potential for success to justify further investment of time, resources, and capital.

- Consider pivoting or refining your startup idea based on research findings to better align with customer needs and market opportunities.

10. Continuously Validate and Learn:

- Treat validation as an ongoing process, continuously gathering feedback, monitoring market trends, and iterating on your startup idea.

- Stay responsive to evolving customer needs, competitive dynamics, and market conditions by adapting and refining your offering over time.

- Foster a culture of experimentation, learning, and continuous improvement within your organization to drive innovation and success.

In conclusion, validating your startup idea through market research and customer feedback is essential for mitigating risks, identifying opportunities, and increasing the likelihood of success. By systematically gathering, analyzing, and applying insights from potential customers, entrepreneurs can make informed decisions, refine their offerings, and create products or services that truly resonate with their target audience.

- Creating a scalable business model that drives profitability and growth

Creating a scalable business model that drives profitability and growth is essential for startups to achieve sustainable success and maximize their potential in the long term. A scalable business model allows a company to efficiently grow its revenue without proportionately increasing its costs. Here's a comprehensive discussion of the process:

1. **Understand Scalability:**

   - Scalability refers to the ability of a business to handle growth and increase revenue without a significant increase in costs or resources.

   - A scalable business model is characterized by high profit margins, low variable costs, and the ability to expand operations without linearly increasing expenses.

2. **Identify Revenue Streams:**

   - Analyze potential revenue streams for your business, including product sales, subscription fees, licensing, advertising, and other monetization strategies.

   - Evaluate the scalability of each revenue stream, considering factors such as market demand, pricing flexibility, and cost structure.

3. **Focus on High Margins:**

   - Prioritize revenue streams with high profit margins to maximize profitability and scalability.

- Identify opportunities to increase margins through cost optimization, value-added services, premium pricing, or upselling to existing customers.

4. **Minimize Variable Costs**:

- Minimize variable costs that scale with revenue growth, such as production costs, marketing expenses, and customer acquisition costs.

- Utilize economies of scale, automation, outsourcing, and technology to reduce costs and improve operational efficiency.

5. **Leverage Technology**:

- Utilize technology to streamline operations, automate repetitive tasks, and scale your business more efficiently.

- Invest in scalable software solutions, cloud computing, and digital platforms to support growth and expansion.

6. Design for Growth:

- Design your business processes, systems, and infrastructure with scalability in mind from the outset.

- Build flexible and adaptable systems that can accommodate increasing volumes of transactions, users, and data without significant disruption.

7. Expand Market Reach:

- Identify opportunities to expand your market reach and reach new customer segments or geographic markets.

- Consider strategic partnerships, distribution channels, franchising, or licensing agreements to accelerate growth and scale more quickly.

8. Invest in Customer Success:

- Prioritize customer satisfaction and retention to drive long-term growth and profitability.

- Invest in customer support, relationship management, and product/service enhancements to maximize customer lifetime value and reduce churn.

9. Monitor Key Metrics:

- Monitor key performance indicators (KPIs) to track the scalability and growth of your business.

- Key metrics may include revenue growth rate, customer acquisition cost (CAC), customer lifetime value (CLV), churn rate, and gross margin.

10. Iterate and Adapt:

- Continuously iterate and adapt your business model based on market feedback, competitive dynamics, and changing customer needs.

- Stay agile and responsive to emerging trends, technological advancements, and evolving market conditions to maintain a competitive edge.

11. Plan for Funding:

- Develop a funding strategy to support scalability and growth, considering options such as bootstrapping, angel investors, venture capital, or debt financing.

- Ensure that your business model is attractive to investors by demonstrating a clear path to profitability, scalability, and market dominance.

In conclusion, creating a scalable business model that drives profitability and growth requires strategic planning, efficient operations, and a relentless focus on customer value. By prioritizing high-margin revenue streams, minimizing variable costs, leveraging technology, and designing for growth, startups can build a foundation for long-term success and scalability. Additionally, staying agile, monitoring key metrics, and adapting to market dynamics are essential for sustaining growth and maintaining a competitive advantage in a rapidly changing business landscape.

- Establishing key metrics and milestones to measure progress and success

Establishing key metrics and milestones to measure progress and success is essential for startups to track their performance, identify areas for improvement, and make informed strategic decisions. By defining clear and actionable metrics, entrepreneurs can gauge their progress toward achieving business objectives and ensure alignment with long-term goals. Here's a comprehensive discussion of the process:

1. **Define Business Objectives:**

   - Start by clearly defining your startup's overarching business objectives and long-term goals. These may include revenue targets, market share growth, customer acquisition goals, profitability thresholds, or product development milestones.

- Ensure that your objectives are specific, measurable, achievable, relevant, and time-bound (SMART) to provide clear direction and focus.

2. Identify Key Performance Indicators (KPIs):

- Identify key performance indicators (KPIs) that directly align with your business objectives and measure critical aspects of your startup's performance.

- Choose KPIs that are relevant, actionable, and indicative of progress and success. Examples include revenue growth rate, customer acquisition cost (CAC), customer lifetime value (CLV), churn rate, gross margin, and conversion rate.

3. Segment Metrics by Functional Areas:

- Segment your KPIs by functional areas of your business, such as marketing, sales, operations, finance, and customer success.

- Define specific metrics for each functional area that reflect its unique goals, challenges, and contribution to overall business success.

4. **Establish Baseline Metrics:**

- Establish baseline metrics to benchmark your startup's performance and track progress over time.

- Use historical data, industry benchmarks, and competitive analysis to set realistic targets and expectations for each metric.

5. **Set Short-term and Long-term Milestones:**

- Break down your business objectives into short-term and long-term milestones that serve as checkpoints for progress and success.

- Set achievable milestones that provide incremental steps toward larger goals, allowing you to celebrate achievements and maintain momentum.

6. Monitor and Track Progress Regularly:

- Implement systems and processes to monitor and track your KPIs regularly, such as weekly, monthly, or quarterly reviews.

- Utilize data analytics tools, dashboards, and reports to visualize and analyze performance trends, identify outliers, and uncover insights.

7. Evaluate and Interpret Data:

- Regularly evaluate and interpret your performance data to assess progress, identify areas of strength and weakness, and pinpoint opportunities for improvement.

- Analyze trends, correlations, and causations to understand the drivers behind changes in your KPIs and make data-driven decisions.

8. Adjust Strategies and Tactics:

- Use insights from your performance metrics to adjust strategies, tactics, and resource allocations as needed.

- Double down on activities and initiatives that drive positive outcomes and pivot or discontinue efforts that fail to deliver desired results.

9. Communicate Progress and Success:

- Communicate progress and success to stakeholders, including team members, investors, advisors, and partners.

- Celebrate achievements, share learnings, and reinforce alignment with overarching business objectives to foster transparency and accountability.

10. Iterate and Refine:

- Continuously iterate and refine your metrics and milestones based on evolving business goals, market dynamics, and organizational priorities.

- Stay agile and responsive to changes in the competitive landscape, customer preferences, and external factors that may impact your startup's performance.

In conclusion, establishing key metrics and milestones is essential for startups to measure progress and success effectively. By defining clear objectives, identifying relevant KPIs, setting achievable milestones, and monitoring performance regularly, entrepreneurs can track their startup's performance, make data-driven decisions, and stay focused on achieving long-term success. Additionally, regular evaluation, adjustment, and communication ensure that metrics and milestones remain aligned with evolving business goals and priorities, driving continuous improvement and growth.

CHAPTER 4:
FUNDRAISING
STRATEGIES FOR
STARTUP SUCCESS

In the dynamic world of entrepreneurship, securing adequate funding is often a critical factor in the success or failure of a startup venture. Chapter: Fundraising Strategies for Startup Success is dedicated to providing aspiring entrepreneurs with actionable insights, practical tips, and proven strategies for navigating the fundraising landscape and securing the capital needed to fuel their growth and innovation.

Fundraising is not merely about raising money; it's about building relationships, articulating a compelling vision, and demonstrating the potential for significant returns on investment. In this chapter, we delve into the intricacies of fundraising, offering guidance on how to approach investors, craft compelling pitches, and negotiate favorable terms.

We begin by exploring the various sources of funding available to startups, from bootstrapping and crowdfunding to angel investors, venture capital, and corporate partnerships. We discuss the advantages and disadvantages of each funding option and provide insights into how to choose the right funding strategy based on your startup's stage of growth, industry, and objectives.

Moreover, we delve into the art of crafting a persuasive pitch deck and delivering a compelling pitch that captures the attention of investors and inspires confidence in your vision. We offer practical tips on how to distill your business idea into a clear and compelling narrative, articulate your value proposition, and address potential concerns or objections.

Furthermore, we explore the nuances of negotiating deal terms, valuing your startup, and structuring investment agreements to ensure a win-win outcome for both parties. We discuss common terms and clauses found in investment agreements, such as valuation, equity ownership, board representation, and investor rights, and offer guidance on how to navigate these negotiations effectively.

Throughout this chapter, we emphasize the importance of building relationships with investors, cultivating trust, and maintaining transparency throughout the fundraising process. We recognize that fundraising is not a one-time event but rather an ongoing effort that requires persistence, resilience, and strategic thinking.

Whether you're a first-time entrepreneur seeking seed funding or a seasoned founder looking to scale your startup to new heights, this chapter serves as a comprehensive guide to fundraising success. Join us as we embark on this journey to unlock the capital needed to fuel your startup's growth, innovation, and ultimate success in the competitive world of entrepreneurship.

- Navigating the funding landscape: from bootstrapping to venture capital

Navigating the funding landscape is a critical aspect of startup success, requiring entrepreneurs to understand and leverage various funding options available at different stages of their journey. From bootstrapping, where founders rely on personal funds and revenue to sustain their business, to venture capital, where external investors provide substantial funding in exchange for equity, each funding source offers unique advantages and considerations. Here's a comprehensive discussion of navigating the funding landscape:

1. Bootstrapping:

   - Bootstrapping involves funding a startup using personal savings, revenue generated from early sales, or resources obtained without external investment.

  - **Advantages**: Bootstrapping offers founders full control over their business, avoids dilution of ownership, and fosters resourcefulness and frugality.

  - **Considerations:** Bootstrapping may limit the speed and scale of growth, require founders to wear multiple hats, and increase personal financial risk.

2. Friends and Family Funding:

  - Friends and family funding involves raising capital from personal connections, such as relatives, friends, or acquaintances, who believe in the founder's vision.

  - **Advantages:** Friends and family funding provides access to capital with fewer strings attached, allows for flexible terms, and can be obtained relatively quickly.

  - **Considerations:** Friends and family funding may strain personal relationships if the business fails, requires clear communication and expectations, and lacks expertise and due diligence typical of professional investors.

3. **Angel Investors:**

- Angel investors are affluent individuals who provide capital to startups in exchange for equity ownership, often in the early stages of development.

- **Advantages:** Angel investors offer expertise, mentorship, and valuable connections in addition to capital, enable rapid growth and market validation, and fill the gap between friends and family funding and institutional investors.

- **Considerations:** Angel investment rounds may involve dilution of founder ownership, negotiation of terms, and alignment of expectations between investors and founders.

4. **Venture Capital (VC):**

- Venture capital firms invest institutional capital in startups with high growth potential in exchange for equity, typically at later stages of development.

- **Advantages:** Venture capital provides substantial funding to scale operations, enter new markets, and accelerate growth, offer access to industry expertise and networks, and validate market potential.

- **Considerations:** Venture capital rounds involve significant dilution, rigorous due diligence, and high expectations for growth and returns, as well as potential loss of control and pressure to achieve aggressive milestones.

5. **Corporate Venture Capital (CVC):**

- Corporate venture capital involves investment from established corporations seeking strategic partnerships, innovation, or access to emerging technologies.

- **Advantages:** Corporate venture capital offers access to industry expertise, distribution channels, and potential strategic partnerships, as well as validation of market potential and credibility.

- **Considerations**: Corporate venture capital may involve conflicts of interest, strategic alignment challenges, and potential loss of independence, as well as differences in investment timelines and decision-making processes compared to traditional VCs.

6. Crowdfunding:

- Crowdfunding platforms enable startups to raise capital from a large number of individual investors or backers in exchange for rewards, equity, or debt.

- **Advantages:** Crowdfunding provides access to capital from a diverse pool of investors, validates market demand and product-market fit, and generates buzz and brand awareness.

- **Considerations:** Crowdfunding campaigns require preparation, marketing, and campaign management, may result in public scrutiny and accountability, and require fulfillment of rewards or obligations to backers.

7. Accelerators and Incubators:

- Accelerator and incubator programs offer startups access to mentorship, resources, and capital in exchange for equity, typically over a fixed duration.

- **Advantages**: Accelerators and incubators provide structured programs, mentorship, and access to networks and investors, accelerate growth and market entry, and validate business models.

- **Considerations**: Accelerator and incubator programs may involve relinquishing equity and accepting standardized terms, require commitment and participation in program activities, and vary in quality and relevance to specific industries and business models.

8. **Government Grants and Incentives:**

- Government grants, subsidies, and incentives provide financial support to startups for research and development, innovation, and job creation, often without equity dilution.

- **Advantages:** Government funding offers non-dilutive capital, supports innovation and economic development, and may provide tax credits or incentives for specific activities or industries.

- **Considerations**: Government grants require compliance with eligibility criteria, application processes, and reporting requirements, may involve long approval timelines and administrative burdens, and vary by jurisdiction and program availability.

In conclusion, navigating the funding landscape requires careful consideration of the stage of startup development, funding requirements, growth objectives, and alignment with investor expectations. By understanding the advantages, considerations, and implications of each funding option—from bootstrapping to venture capital—entrepreneurs can make informed decisions, leverage available resources, and secure the capital needed to fuel their growth and success. Additionally, diversifying funding sources, building relationships with investors, and maintaining transparency and accountability throughout the fundraising process are essential for long-term sustainability and resilience in the competitive startup ecosystem.

- Crafting a compelling pitch deck and effectively communicating your startup's vision

Crafting a compelling pitch deck and effectively communicating your startup's vision is crucial for attracting investors, partners, and customers, as well as building credibility and generating excitement around your venture. A well-crafted pitch deck serves as a visual representation of your business idea, highlighting key elements of your startup's value proposition, market opportunity, team, and traction. Here's a comprehensive discussion of how to create a compelling pitch deck and effectively communicate your startup's vision:

1. **Understand Your Audience:**

   - Tailor your pitch deck to the specific needs, interests, and preferences of your audience, whether they are investors, potential partners, customers, or stakeholders.

   - Research your audience's background, expertise, and investment criteria to ensure that your pitch resonates with their priorities and objectives.

2. **Define Your Value Proposition:**

   - Clearly articulate your startup's value proposition—the unique benefits, solutions, or advantages it offers to customers or users.

   - Identify the problem or pain point your product or service addresses, the solution it provides, and the value it delivers to customers.

3. **Tell a Compelling Story:**

   - Craft a narrative that captures the essence of your startup's vision, mission, and journey.

- Use storytelling techniques to engage your audience emotionally, build rapport, and make your pitch memorable and impactful.

4. Structure Your Pitch Deck:

- Structure your pitch deck logically and intuitively, following a consistent flow that guides your audience through the key elements of your business.

- Typically, a pitch deck includes slides covering the problem, solution, market opportunity, business model, traction, team, competition, and ask (funding or next steps).

5. Focus on Visual Appeal:

- Use visuals, graphics, and imagery to enhance the visual appeal of your pitch deck and reinforce key messages.

- Keep slides clean, uncluttered, and visually consistent, using fonts, colors, and layouts that align with your brand identity.

6. Keep It Concise and Impactful:

- Keep your pitch deck concise, focusing on conveying essential information and avoiding unnecessary details or jargon.

- Aim for brevity and clarity, using bullet points, visuals, and headlines to convey key points succinctly.

7. Highlight Market Opportunity:

- Clearly define the size, growth potential, and dynamics of your target market, emphasizing the opportunity for disruption, innovation, or expansion.

- Provide evidence of market validation, such as customer testimonials, industry reports, or traction metrics.

8. Demonstrate Traction and Progress:

- Showcase evidence of traction, progress, or milestones achieved to date, such as user growth, revenue metrics, partnerships, or product development milestones.

- Highlight key achievements and milestones that validate your startup's viability, progress, and momentum.

9. Introduce Your Team:

- Introduce key members of your team, highlighting their expertise, experience, and roles within the company.

- Emphasize the strengths, qualifications, and relevant achievements of each team member, showcasing the collective talent and capabilities driving your startup forward.

10. Address Potential Objections:

- Anticipate and address potential objections or concerns that investors or stakeholders may have about your startup, product, or market opportunity.

- Provide thoughtful responses, evidence, or mitigation strategies to alleviate doubts and build confidence in your ability to execute your vision.

11. Practice and Refine Delivery:

- Practice delivering your pitch deck multiple times, refining your delivery, timing, and emphasis to ensure clarity, confidence, and impact.

- Solicit feedback from mentors, advisors, or peers, and iterate on your pitch based on their input and observations.

12. End with a Clear Call to Action:

- Conclude your pitch with a clear call to action, specifying the next steps you want your audience to take, whether it's scheduling a follow-up meeting, making an investment, or trying your product/service.

In conclusion, crafting a compelling pitch deck and effectively communicating your startup's vision requires a strategic approach, clear messaging, and attention to detail. By understanding your audience, defining your value proposition, telling a compelling story, and structuring your pitch deck effectively, you can capture the attention of investors, partners, and customers, and inspire confidence in your startup's potential for success. Additionally, practicing delivery, soliciting feedback, and iterating on your pitch deck is essential for refining your message and maximizing impact.

- Building relationships with investors and securing funding to fuel growth and expansion

Building relationships with investors and securing funding to fuel growth and expansion is a crucial aspect of startup success. Establishing strong connections with investors requires trust, transparency, and alignment of interests while securing funding involves effectively articulating your startup's value proposition, demonstrating market opportunity, and showcasing traction and potential for growth. Here's a comprehensive discussion of how to build relationships with investors and secure funding:

1. Identify Target Investors:

- Research and identify potential investors who have a track record of investing in startups in your industry, stage, and geographic region.

- Consider factors such as investment focus, portfolio companies, investment thesis, and network connections when identifying target investors.

2. Build a Network:

- Attend networking events, industry conferences, and startup pitch competitions to meet and connect with investors, entrepreneurs, and industry professionals.

- Leverage online platforms, such as LinkedIn, AngelList, and startup accelerators, to expand your network and reach potential investors.

3. Establish Credibility and Trust:

- Demonstrate credibility and integrity by being transparent, responsive, and reliable in your communications and interactions with investors.

- Showcase your expertise, domain knowledge, and track record of success in your industry or relevant field to build confidence and trust.

4. Engage in Relationship Building:

- Take a relational approach to building connections with investors, focusing on long-term relationships rather than transactional interactions.

- Invest time in getting to know investors personally, understanding their investment preferences, objectives, and risk tolerance, and tailoring your approach accordingly.

5. Develop a Compelling Investment Thesis:

- Develop a compelling investment thesis that articulates your startup's unique value proposition, market opportunity, competitive advantage, and potential for growth and profitability.

- Tailor your investment thesis to resonate with the interests, priorities, and investment criteria of target investors, addressing key questions and concerns they may have.

6. Craft an Effective Pitch Deck:

- Create a visually appealing and informative pitch deck that effectively communicates your startup's vision, mission, value proposition, market opportunity, traction, team, and financial projections.

- Tailor your pitch deck to different investor audiences, highlighting relevant aspects of your business and addressing specific interests or concerns.

7. Demonstrate Traction and Progress:

- Showcase evidence of traction, progress, and milestones achieved to date, such as user growth, revenue metrics, partnerships, product development milestones, or customer testimonials.

- Provide tangible proof points that validate your startup's market fit, customer demand, and potential for scalability and profitability.

8. Negotiate Terms and Structure:

- Negotiate investment terms and structure that align with your startup's objectives, valuation, and growth trajectory, while also meeting the expectations and requirements of investors.

- Seek legal and financial advice to navigate complex terms and agreements, ensuring clarity, fairness, and compliance with regulatory requirements.

9. Maintain Communication and Transparency:

- Maintain open and transparent communication with investors throughout the fundraising process and beyond, providing regular updates on progress, challenges, and milestones.

- Foster a culture of trust and collaboration by soliciting feedback, addressing concerns, and demonstrating accountability in managing investor funds and achieving business objectives.

10. **Leverage Investor Networks and Resources:**

- Leverage investor networks and resources to access additional funding, strategic partnerships, industry connections, and mentorship opportunities.

- Seek introductions and referrals from existing investors, advisors, or industry contacts to expand your network and reach new potential investors.

11. **Stay Resilient and Persistent:**

- Recognize that securing funding can be a challenging and time-consuming process, requiring resilience, perseverance, and determination.

- Stay persistent in pursuing opportunities, following up with investors, and iterating on your approach based on feedback and lessons learned.

12. **Celebrate Success and Milestones:**

- Celebrate successful fundraising rounds, milestones achieved, and progress made toward your startup's goals, acknowledging the support and contributions of investors and stakeholders.

- Maintain an optimistic outlook, while also remaining focused on executing your growth strategy and delivering value to customers and shareholders.

In conclusion, building relationships with investors and securing funding requires a strategic and proactive approach, grounded in trust, credibility, and effective communication. By identifying target investors, developing a compelling investment thesis, demonstrating traction and progress, and maintaining transparency throughout the fundraising process, startups can attract investment capital to fuel growth and expansion. Additionally, leveraging investor networks, staying resilient and persistent, and celebrating successes along the way is essential for building long-term partnerships and achieving sustainable growth and success.

CHAPTER 5: SCALING FOR SUSTAINABLE GROWTH

Scaling a startup for sustainable growth is a transformative journey that requires strategic planning, operational excellence, and unwavering commitment to delivering value to customers and stakeholders. Chapter: Scaling for Sustainable Growth is dedicated to exploring the essential strategies, principles, and best practices for scaling startups effectively while maintaining agility, resilience, and long-term viability.

Scaling a startup goes beyond mere expansion; it involves achieving operational efficiency, optimizing processes, and unlocking new opportunities for growth and innovation. In this chapter, we delve into the critical elements of scaling, offering insights into how to navigate the complexities of rapid growth, capitalize on market opportunities, and overcome common challenges encountered along the way.

We begin by examining the foundations of scaling, including establishing scalable business models, building robust infrastructure, and fostering a culture of innovation and continuous improvement. We explore the importance of scalability in driving profitability, attracting investment, and creating sustainable value for customers and stakeholders.

Moreover, we delve into the intricacies of scaling operations, from expanding market reach and penetrating new segments to optimizing supply chain logistics and managing organizational complexity. We discuss strategies for scaling sales and marketing efforts, enhancing customer acquisition and retention, and leveraging technology to automate processes and streamline workflows.

Furthermore, we address the organizational and cultural aspects of scaling, including building high-performing teams, nurturing leadership talent, and fostering a growth mindset throughout the organization. We explore the challenges of scaling culture, communication, and decision-making, and offer practical tips for maintaining alignment, cohesion, and agility as the company grows.

Throughout this chapter, we emphasize the importance of maintaining a customer-centric focus, adapting to evolving market dynamics, and staying true to your startup's core values and vision. We recognize that scaling is not a linear process but rather a dynamic journey characterized by experimentation, iteration, and learning.

Whether you're a founder embarking on the next phase of growth or a leader guiding your team through a period of expansion, this chapter serves as a comprehensive guide to scaling your startup for sustainable success. Join us as we explore the strategies, insights, and best practices for navigating the challenges and opportunities of scaling in today's competitive business landscape.

- Scaling your startup operations while maintaining quality and efficiency

Scaling startup operations while maintaining quality and efficiency is a complex undertaking that requires strategic planning, process optimization, and a focus on delivering value to customers. As startups grow, they face challenges such as increased operational complexity, resource constraints, and maintaining the quality standards that contributed to their initial success. Here's a comprehensive discussion of how to scale startup operations while preserving quality and efficiency:

1. **Evaluate Current Processes and Systems:**

   - Conduct a thorough assessment of your startup's existing processes, systems, and workflows to identify bottlenecks, inefficiencies, and areas for improvement.

- Analyze key performance indicators (KPIs) related to productivity, quality, and customer satisfaction to gauge the effectiveness of current operations.

2. Standardize and Document Processes:

- Standardize and document core processes and workflows to ensure consistency, reliability, and scalability as the company grows.

- Develop clear Standard Operating Procedures (SOPs), guidelines, and training materials to facilitate onboarding of new employees and maintain quality standards.

3. Invest in Technology and Automation:

- Leverage technology and automation tools to streamline repetitive tasks, eliminate manual errors, and improve operational efficiency.

- Implement software solutions for project management, customer relationship management

(CRM), accounting, inventory management, and other key functions to optimize workflows and data management.

4. Focus on Talent Acquisition and Development:

- Invest in recruiting, training, and retaining top talent to support scaling operations and maintain quality standards.

- Hire employees who are aligned with the company culture, values, and vision, and provide ongoing training and professional development opportunities to enhance skills and competencies.

5. Implement Agile and Lean Methodologies:

- Adopt agile and lean methodologies to enhance flexibility, responsiveness, and adaptability in scaling operations.

- Break down projects into smaller, manageable tasks, prioritize work based on value and impact, and iterate on processes based on feedback and lessons learned.

6. Outsource Non-Core Functions:

- Consider outsourcing non-core functions such as accounting, IT support, customer service, or manufacturing to specialized service providers or contractors.

- Focus internal resources on core competencies and strategic initiatives while leveraging external expertise and cost-effective solutions for auxiliary tasks.

7. Maintain a Customer-Centric Focus:

- Prioritize customer satisfaction and retention throughout the scaling process, ensuring that operational changes do not compromise the quality of products or services.

- Solicit feedback from customers, monitor satisfaction metrics, and address issues promptly to maintain trust and loyalty.

8. Implement Quality Assurance Measures:

- Implement robust quality assurance (QA) measures and performance metrics to monitor and evaluate the quality of products or services delivered to customers.

- Establish quality standards, conduct regular audits and inspections, and provide feedback loops for continuous improvement and corrective action.

9. Monitor and Adapt in Real-Time:

- Continuously monitor key performance indicators (KPIs) and operational metrics to track progress, identify trends, and address issues proactively.

- Stay agile and responsive to changes in market conditions, customer preferences, and competitive dynamics, adapting operations accordingly to maintain quality and efficiency.

10. Promote a Culture of Continuous Improvement:

- Foster a culture of continuous improvement, innovation, and learning within the organization, encouraging employees to suggest ideas for enhancing efficiency and quality.

- Celebrate successes, recognize achievements, and incentivize performance improvements to reinforce a culture of excellence and accountability.

11. **Manage Growth Strategically:**

- Manage growth strategically, balancing the pace of expansion with the ability to maintain quality standards and operational efficiency.

- Set realistic growth targets, allocate resources effectively, and prioritize initiatives that have the greatest impact on achieving long-term objectives.

12. **Stay Committed to Your Values and Vision:**

- Stay true to your startup's core values, vision, and mission throughout the scaling process, ensuring that operational changes align with the company's overarching goals and principles.

- Communicate transparently with employees, customers, and stakeholders about the company's values, priorities, and commitments, fostering trust and alignment.

In conclusion, scaling startup operations while maintaining quality and efficiency requires a holistic approach that encompasses process optimization, technology adoption, talent management, and a customer-centric focus. By evaluating current processes, investing in technology and talent, implementing quality assurance measures, and fostering a culture of continuous improvement, startups can scale operations successfully while preserving the quality standards that are essential for long-term success and sustainability. Additionally, staying committed to core values, vision, and customer satisfaction ensures that operational changes contribute to overall growth and competitiveness in the marketplace.

- Building a resilient team culture that fosters innovation and collaboration

Building a resilient team culture that fosters innovation and collaboration is essential for startups to adapt to change, overcome challenges, and thrive in a dynamic business environment. A resilient team culture enables employees to embrace uncertainty, learn from failure, and collaborate effectively to drive innovation and achieve collective goals.

Here's a comprehensive discussion of how to build such a culture:

1. Define Core Values and Purpose:

   - Establish clear core values and a shared purpose that guide the behavior and decision-making of team members.

- Articulate a compelling vision for the company and communicate how each team member contributes to achieving that vision.

2. **Encourage Psychological Safety:**

- Create an environment of psychological safety where team members feel comfortable taking risks, sharing ideas, and expressing their opinions without fear of judgment or reprisal.

- Foster open communication, active listening, and empathy to build trust and mutual respect among team members.

3. **Promote Autonomy and Ownership:**

- Empower team members with autonomy and ownership over their work, allowing them to make decisions, experiment with new ideas, and take initiative.

- Encourage a culture of accountability where individuals take responsibility for their actions and outcomes, and celebrate both successes and learning opportunities.

4. Support Continuous Learning and Development:

- Invest in learning and development opportunities to help team members expand their skills, knowledge, and capabilities.

- Provide access to training programs, workshops, conferences, and mentorship to foster personal and professional growth.

5. Embrace Diversity and Inclusion:

- Embrace diversity and inclusion by fostering a culture that values and celebrates differences in background, perspective, and experience.

- Create opportunities for diverse voices to be heard, contribute ideas, and participate in decision-making processes.

6. Encourage Collaboration and Cross-Functional Teams:

- Encourage collaboration and teamwork by breaking down silos and promoting cross-functional interactions and projects.

- Foster a spirit of collaboration by recognizing and rewarding teamwork, sharing credit for achievements, and promoting a "we-first" mentality.

7. Provide Resources and Support:

- Provide the resources, tools, and support necessary for team members to succeed in their roles and projects.

- Remove barriers to collaboration and innovation by ensuring access to necessary technology, information, and support services.

8. Celebrate Creativity and Experimentation:

- Encourage creativity and experimentation by creating space for brainstorming, ideation, and prototyping.

- Celebrate both successes and failures as opportunities for learning and growth, and encourage a culture of experimentation and continuous improvement.

9. Lead by Example:

- Lead by example by demonstrating resilience, adaptability, and a growth mindset in your behavior and actions.

- Model the values and behaviors you want to see in your team and provide mentorship and guidance to support their development.

10. Promote Work-Life Balance and Well-Being:

- Promote work-life balance and well-being by encouraging healthy habits, prioritizing mental and physical health, and providing resources for stress management and self-care.

- Recognize the importance of holistic well-being in fostering resilience and creativity in the workplace.

11. Solicit Feedback and Iterate:

- Solicit feedback from team members regularly to assess the effectiveness of team culture initiatives and identify areas for improvement.

- Iterate on team culture initiatives based on feedback and insights, and be open to making adjustments to better meet the needs of your team.

12. Celebrate Successes and Milestones:

- Celebrate successes, milestones, and achievements as a team to foster a sense of camaraderie, pride, and motivation.

- Recognize and reward individual and team contributions to innovation, collaboration, and achieving shared goals.

In conclusion, building a resilient team culture that fosters innovation and collaboration requires intentional effort, leadership commitment, and ongoing reinforcement of core values and behaviors. By creating an environment of psychological safety, promoting autonomy and ownership, supporting continuous learning and development, and embracing diversity and inclusion, startups can cultivate a culture that empowers employees to adapt, innovate, and thrive in the face of adversity. Additionally, promoting collaboration, providing resources and support, and leading by example are essential for building a resilient team culture that drives long-term success and sustainability.

- Leveraging technology and data-driven insights to optimize processes and drive continuous improvement

Leveraging technology and data-driven insights to optimize processes and drive continuous improvement is crucial for startups seeking to enhance efficiency, productivity, and innovation. By harnessing the power of technology and leveraging data analytics, startups can identify inefficiencies, streamline workflows, and make informed decisions to drive operational excellence and sustainable growth. Here's a comprehensive discussion on how startups can effectively leverage technology and data-driven insights:

1. Identify Pain Points and Opportunities:

- Conduct a thorough assessment of existing processes and workflows to identify pain points, bottlenecks, and areas for improvement.

- Prioritize areas where technology and data-driven insights can have the greatest impact on efficiency, quality, and customer satisfaction.

2. Implement Technology Solutions:

- Invest in technology solutions that address specific needs and objectives, such as project management software, CRM systems, workflow automation tools, and data analytics platforms.

- Select technology solutions that are scalable, user-friendly, and customizable to meet the unique requirements of your startup.

3. Automate Repetitive Tasks:

- Identify repetitive tasks and manual processes that can be automated using technology solutions.

- Implement workflow automation tools, robotic process automation (RPA), and artificial intelligence (AI) technologies to streamline routine tasks, reduce errors, and free up time for higher-value activities.

4. Integrate Systems and Applications:

- Integrate disparate systems and applications to create a unified and seamless workflow across different departments and functions.

- Adopt integration platforms or APIs (Application Programming Interfaces) to facilitate data exchange and communication between various systems and applications.

5. Utilize Data Analytics:

- Collect, analyze, and interpret data to gain actionable insights into business performance, customer behavior, market trends, and operational efficiency.

- Implement data analytics tools and techniques, such as business intelligence (BI) dashboards, predictive analytics, and machine learning algorithms, to extract meaningful insights from large datasets.

6. Monitor Key Performance Indicators (KPIs):

- Define key performance indicators (KPIs) relevant to your business objectives and use them to track progress, measure performance, and identify areas for improvement.

- Establish benchmarks and targets for KPIs and leverage data analytics to monitor performance trends, detect anomalies, and take corrective actions as needed.

7. Optimize Decision-Making:

- Make data-driven decisions based on objective analysis and insights rather than intuition or anecdotal evidence.

- Implement data-driven decision-making processes across the organization, ensuring that stakeholders have access to timely, accurate, and relevant information to inform their decisions.

8. Predictive Maintenance and Optimization:

- Implement predictive maintenance strategies using IoT (Internet of Things) sensors, predictive analytics, and machine learning algorithms to anticipate equipment failures and optimize maintenance schedules.

- Leverage data-driven insights to optimize resource allocation, improve asset utilization, and reduce downtime and maintenance costs.

9. Facilitate Continuous Improvement:

- Foster a culture of continuous improvement by encouraging employees to identify opportunities for optimization, experimentation, and innovation.

- Implement feedback mechanisms, suggestion programs, and cross-functional collaboration to solicit ideas and insights from employees at all levels of the organization.

10. Iterate and Adapt:

- Continuously iterate processes, workflows, and technology solutions based on feedback, insights, and changing business needs.

- Be agile and adaptive in responding to emerging trends, market dynamics, and technological advancements to stay ahead of the curve and maintain competitiveness.

11. Invest in Employee Training and Development:

- Provide training and upskilling opportunities to employees to ensure they have the necessary skills and knowledge to leverage technology and data-driven insights effectively.

- Foster a learning culture where employees are encouraged to explore new technologies, acquire new skills, and stay abreast of industry best practices.

12. Ensure Data Security and Compliance:

- Implement robust data security measures and protocols to protect sensitive information and maintain compliance with relevant regulations and industry standards.

- Ensure data integrity, confidentiality, and availability through encryption, access controls, regular audits, and adherence to data privacy regulations.

In conclusion, leveraging technology and data-driven insights to optimize processes and drive continuous improvement is essential for startups to achieve operational excellence, innovation, and competitive advantage. By investing in technology solutions, harnessing the power of data analytics, and fostering a culture of continuous improvement, startups can streamline workflows, enhance efficiency, and unlock new opportunities for growth and success. Additionally, promoting data-driven decision-making, facilitating employee training and development, and ensuring data security and compliance are essential for maximizing the benefits of technology and data-driven insights while mitigating risks and challenges.

CONCLUSION

In conclusion, "Startup Strategies: Navigating Success in the New Business Landscape" serves as a comprehensive guide for entrepreneurs embarking on the exhilarating journey of startup creation and growth in today's dynamic business environment. Throughout this book, we have explored the essential strategies, principles, and best practices for navigating the complexities of the modern business landscape, from understanding market dynamics to scaling operations and securing funding.

In a world characterized by rapid technological advancements, shifting consumer behaviors, and evolving market trends, startups face both unprecedented opportunities and formidable challenges. However, armed with the insights, tools, and frameworks provided in this book, entrepreneurs can confidently navigate the uncertainties of the startup journey and position their ventures for long-term success.

We have emphasized the importance of embracing innovation, agility, and adaptability as core tenets of startup success. By fostering a culture of creativity, resilience, and continuous learning, startups can effectively respond to market changes, capitalize on emerging opportunities, and stay ahead of the competition.

Furthermore, we have underscored the critical role of collaboration, mentorship, and community in supporting startup growth and development. By leveraging the collective wisdom and experiences of peers, advisors, and industry experts, entrepreneurs can accelerate their learning curve, avoid common pitfalls, and make informed decisions that drive sustainable growth.

As we conclude this journey together, I encourage you, the reader, to reflect on the insights and strategies presented in this book and apply them to your own entrepreneurial endeavors. Whether you are a budding entrepreneur just starting out or a seasoned founder looking to take your startup to the next level, remember that success is not merely defined by financial metrics or market dominance, but by the impact you create, the relationships you build, and the legacy you leave behind.

May this book serve as a valuable resource and companion on your entrepreneurial journey, empowering you to navigate the ever-changing business landscape with confidence, resilience, and purpose? Here's to the bold visionaries, the relentless innovators, and the courageous dreamers who dare to challenge the status quo and shape the future of entrepreneurship. Together, let us continue to forge new paths, inspire change, and unlock the limitless potential of the startup ecosystem.